Wandering Woman: Oklahoma

The Ultimate Road Trip: One Woman's Journey Across the United States by RV

Julie Bettendorf

Contents

Introduction

"Not all who wander are lost." **JRR Tolkien**

Are you sure? I thought to myself, as I tried not to panic. I was a long way from anything familiar, but that was how it should be. I had driven thousands of miles on dusty, pothole-filled roads. It's often on the worst roads that you can discover something truly amazing.

My dusty CRV was parked beside me, containing one restless dog and a variety of snack bags, all empty by now. There were no buildings in sight, no cars or people or movement at all. Only the constant humming of the insects as they buzzed around my head.

I turned to my left – another straight road that trailed off into the distance. I glanced over to the right, then behind me – two more barely discernible roads stretched out into the abyss. I was in a four-way intersection with no signs, no sense of direction, and no sign of life for several miles. No cell service either. *Damn*, I thought. *I'm lost.*

How did I get here? I couldn't help but feel like this little intersection was a cruel metaphor for life. I began to daydream, imagining each road might transport me back to a different time, a different role in my life, and a different me.

If I took the road from whence I came, it could lead me all the way back to Oregon, back to my cheating third husband, back to a life of loneliness and solitude. There is no greater loneliness than being married to someone who isn't actually present in your life.

If I took the road to my left, perhaps it could take me back to my career as a dental hygienist, a job I hated deep down in my soul. There is something so disengaging about cleaning teeth for a living. It's a disgusting, smelly way to get a paycheck. It pays well, which is great, but the best part is the huge gob of friends I enjoy to this day.

Or maybe the road to my right, *yes – maybe that's the path*, I imagined. Maybe it could take me back to my real treasure, my kids. Back to their smiling, innocent faces as toddlers, as they danced around the Christmas tree and their father and I were still married. Back when they still needed me for every little thing.

But, that was just it. I didn't feel needed anymore. My kids weren't toddlers anymore – they were both full-grown adults, and far too busy for me. My dental buddies were still working, but I wasn't. Dental hygiene had robbed me of the cartilage in my fingers, giving me severe, disabling arthritis. And, I wouldn't be returning to any more husbands either, because three marriages were quite enough for me.

All three of these paths, all three of these roles – the wife, the mother, and the dental hygienist – had seemingly been stripped from me within a year. I was lost and looking to find myself again.

The funny thing about this phrase, "not all who wander are lost" – is that, in my experience, wandering and being lost walk hand-in-hand with one another, and the expression can be flipped. In my experience, not all who are lost are wandering, and that is a real disservice to the beauty and clarity that the world has to offer.

When one becomes lost, wandering is the only option to guide oneself back to a path. After all, one could not come upon any dirt path at all without wandering.

I began wandering at an early age, both with my mind and with my feet. At eight years old, I was reading a book about archaeology and dreaming of one day seeing Egypt. I didn't follow a traditional path in high school either, going heavily into foreign languages, in hopes of one day using them.

At twenty-five years old, I divorced my first husband (the dental student who talked me into becoming a dental hygienist so I could work for him) and decided to give traveling a real shot. I took off for the Andes and Macchu Picchu, climbing up ancient Inca stone steps to reach the magnificent ruins.

Anyone who has been to Macchu Picchu will tell you there is something ethereal and deeply spiritual about the place. The ruins stretch out across the emerald green mountains, way up in the middle of the sky. Macchu Picchu gave me my first experience of feeling history. This trip inspired me to come back and complete a degree in archaeology, and I've been wandering ever since.

More travel followed including a backpack trip around Europe for three months, by myself, and trips to Britain, Italy, and Greece. I visited the burial places of Crusaders, mummies, and ancient kings. I happened upon the castle of my namesake in Bettendorf, Luxembourg, and wandered my way through European history.

My favorite excursion by far was finally seeing Egypt with my daughter in 2012. Just like my childhood dream envisioned, I rode a camel beneath the pyramids of Giza, with my head wrapped in some man's sweaty turban. It was perfect.

Traveling has always been my own personal antidote to pain. I went to Mexico after my first and second divorces, Canada after my third, and Italy after my dad died. Call it avoidance if you want, but I call it an accelerated form of healing in the purest sense of the word. I believe travel can heal your soul.

Wandering has always worked its wonders on me – made me feel renewed, rejoiceful, grateful, and purposeful. It's been my medicine.

So, as I stood in that intersection, I once again wondered how wandering had led me so astray this time. *What the hell am I supposed to do now?* It was then that I realized that one last path had not been considered yet – the path which stretched straight out in front of me. *Which role does this represent?* I pondered.

The answer smacked me in the face.

That last dirt road – the only path that could take me where I wanted to go, the only path that ever truly healed me or showed me the way – was the path of the traveler. The wife, the mother, and the hygienist roles – though valued in their time – were sitting in the bleachers now. It was time to welcome and enable my boldest, bravest, and perhaps most pivotal role yet:

The role of the Wandering Woman.

Welcome to Wandering Woman

This book is for you – the grieving empty nester mom, the begrudged housewife, the woman in need of a drastic change in her life. Really, this book is for anyone with a passion for traveling. If you feel lost with no sense of direction or purpose in life, that's a bonus – this book will be even more appealing to you. And lastly, if you're a man reading this book, congratulations for holding a book with the word woman in the title. You're contributing to gender equality, and that's pretty neat.

I decided to combine three of my dearest loves – travel, history, and archaeology – and put them into a book because I believe wandering has the power to change your life. I have been to many areas of the world and have enjoyed too many outstanding experiences to list. However, by the time both my children moved out in 2017, I realized I was a stranger in my own country. It was the perfect time to explore a new country (my own) and discover a new me at the same time. I have been traveling for five years now, and I've upgraded to a small RV. I also have a new traveling companion, another sweet Sheltie, named Rosie. **Wandering Woman** is the chronicle of my journey across the United States, discovering the joy of getting lost and finding myself along the way.

Why You Need to Take a Road Trip

*A**merica, the beautiful?*** I sure think so, but I didn't realize just how beautiful our country is until I embarked on traveling across the United States, full time, in a small RV.

The United States offers something for everyone. From spectacular beaches, austere mountains, to rolling plains, our country has it all. It's difficult to comprehend just how large and impressive our scenery is, until you experience it first-hand, with the ultimate road trip.

I also realized just how much of our history is missing from U.S. history I was taught as a kid. The history of our country didn't begin with the pilgrims landing on Plymouth Rock in the 1600s. Our history is far more ancient, with rock art and archaeological sites dating back over 12,000 years.

We owe a tremendous debt to early pioneers who tamed our land. The Mormons and other groups ventured into the great unknown with their families and their worldly possessions. Some of them pulled cumbersome handcarts across the country to settle in inhospitable, dangerous locations.

The goal of **Wandering Woman** is to bring history back to life and make it interesting again. I am presenting some famous sites, and many little-known ones. You will take the road-less-traveled with me, while we explore ghost towns, rock art sites, archaeological sites, and museums, to discover the colorful tapestry that is our country.

I present some history, including dates, but my goal is to present more of the real-life stories of history, including ghost stories, profiles in history, voices from the past, and moments in time, to give you, the reader, a deeper understanding of the context of history.

This is by no means an exhaustive list of places to visit. In fact, I encourage you to discover America for yourself, as I am doing, by making a trek across the land by car or RV. You can venture forth as the early explorers did, just a little more comfortably, with a lot less hardship.

I hope you enjoy this book and take a little time out to discover our beautiful country, and maybe even discover yourself in the process.

Safe Travels,

Julie Bettendorf

Welcome to Oklahoma

The Sooner State

*O*klahoma has played an important part in history, from ancient cultures like those who built the Spiro Mounds, to the Oklahoma Land Run of 1889, which led to the settlement of the state. Oklahoma was also home to historical figures, like the Doolin gang, who shot it out at Ingalls. Today, you can enjoy Oklahoma's history, vast amounts of land, and the friendly smiles of people who live there.

Five things to love about Oklahoma:

- Charming historic towns like Guthrie

- The ancient history of places like Spiro Mounds

- Acres and acres of rich farmland that help to feed us all

- The stunning beauty of places like Sacred Heart Mission

- Random, slow moving tortoises trying to cross the road

Dreams of Oklahoma

"My mom grew up in poverty in Oklahoma - like Dust Bowl, nine people in one room kind of place - and the way she got out of poverty was through education. My dad grew up without a dad, with very little and he also made his way out through education." **Jennifer Garner**

"My first real job, I sold Christmas trees when I was twelve for extra money. I did that until I was fifteen. Then I bagged groceries, and I worked at the first Borders ever in Tulsa, Oklahoma." **Bill Hader**

"I grew up in Oklahoma and Missouri, and I just loved film. My folks would take us to the drive-in on summer nights, and we'd sit on the hood of the car. I just had this profound love for storytelling." **Brad Pitt**

Famous Citizens of Oklahoma

Gene Autry (1907–1998), actor, musician, Major League Baseball team owner

Gary Busey (born 1944), actor

Lon Chaney Jr (1906–1973), actor

Joan Crawford (1906–1977), Academy Award-winning actress

James Garner (1928–2014), actor

Ron Howard (born 1954), director, producer, actor

Tom Mix (1880-1940), cowboy star of silent films

Brad Pitt (born 1963), actor and producer

Will Rogers (1875–1935), actor, columnist, radio personality

Wes Studi (born 1947), actor

Early Oklahoma

Early Oklahoma Cowboy

Early Oklahoma Hotel

Early Doaksville

Guthrie

*G**uthrie** has a beautiful, very walkable old town with many outstanding brick buildings from the 1890s. What began as a railroad station stop in 1887, emerged as a developed town. 10,000

new residents came into Guthrie after the Oklahoma Land Run in 1889. Guthrie became the first capitol of the Oklahoma Territory.

Today, the Guthrie Historic District is known for over 2000 buildings from the late 19th and early 20th centuries. Some of the historic buildings in Guthrie include the Santa Fe Depot, with the only railroad service into Oklahoma Territory during the Oklahoma Land Run. The current depot building was built in 1903.

There are many ornate buildings in Guthrie, including the DeFord Building, built in 1890. Irwin DeFord, an early money-lender and capitalist, lived on an upper floor in the building.

The Same Old Moses Saloon has one of the more colorful stories in Guthrie. Moses Weinberger came to Guthrie from Kansas
and started out selling bananas. He decided selling alcohol would
make more money than selling fruit, so he opened the Same Old
Moses Saloon. The Same Old Moses was plagued by visits from
Carry Nation, a famous prohibitionist, who swung her hatchet at
Weinberger's saloon.

The Bonfils Building is another building from the 1890s with a unique history. F.C. Bonfils joined the Land Run when he was 28. He was a descendant of Napoleon. Bonfils was also a con artist who constructed a money making machine which people bought, hoping to turn small bills into larger ones. Bonfils was forced out of Guthrie and settled in Denver, where he died a wealthy man.

The De Steiguer Building, built in the 1890s, was built by the Louis and Rodolph De Steiguer brothers, two pioneers in banking. It's unusual because it is actually two separate buildings, designed to look like one building.

The Oklahoma Building, built in 1901, housed the Logan County
Bank and Territorial governors offices. The basement of the huge
building was used as a stable for horses and storage for carriages.

You can also see the Oklahoma Daily Building from 1902, which was home to the first newspaper in Oklahoma Territory and the largest printing plant west of the Mississippi. The site began as a tent during the Land Run, and was replaced by a wooden building, and then by brick.

Among the historic buildings is the Gaffney Building, also built in the 1890s. It houses the amazing Oklahoma Frontier Drugstore Museum. It's a fascinating trip into the past with drugs and drugstore artifacts from the frontier.

Glass bottles of all kinds line the shelves, along with pharmacy antiques, medicaments, and antiseptics from days gone by, all in their original vintage packaging.

The museum also contains an intact soda fountain, complete with vintage metal chairs. It's a wonderful way to spend an hour or two.

Next door you can take a stroll through the peaceful apothecary garden, and learn all about healing herbs and plants.

As you walk around this enjoyable town, don't miss the outdoor jail cell for the Oklahoma Territory.

Guthrie also has a huge, absolutely lovely park with fountains, and lots of charming ducks.

How to get to Guthrie:

Guthrie is located about 36 miles north of Oklahoma City off Interstate 35.

Profiles in history:

Carry, also spelled Carrie, Nation began her life as Carrie Moore, born November 25, 1846, in Kentucky. Carry married David Nation in 1874 and became a notorious member of the temperance movement which opposed alcohol before prohibition. Carry Nation was well known for attacking taverns with a hatchet. One of the taverns she attacked was Same Old Moses in Guthrie. Carry was also known for charitable acts, including starting a shelter for wives and children of alcoholics. Carry Nation died June 9, 1911 in Leavenworth, Kansas.

Elmer McCurdy was born on January 1, 1880, in Washington, Maine. He was an outlaw who was shot and killed in 1911, while robbing a train in Oklahoma. McCurdy became more famous after his death. His body was mummified and put on display in a funeral home in Oklahoma. His body later became an exhibit in traveling carnivals during the 1920s through the 1960s. McCurdy's remains were eventually identified in an amusement park in Long Beach, California. He was finally buried in 1977, at the Summit View Cemetery in Guthrie.

A word about the Oklahoma Land Run

On September 16, 1893, the ***Oklahoma Land Run*** began. Would-be settlers came from hundreds of miles away to claim a parcel of land, farm it, and homestead there. The only catch was, the first person to reach the area could settle the land. The result was a stampede. For the unfortunate people who tried to ride to the parcel before the starting gun, they were shot.

It is estimated about 50,000 people waited for the signal that would start the Land Run. Then, at noon, the cannons sounded, and the Land Run began. Settlers ran for both country lots and city lots. The changes in Guthrie were dramatic, and it became what was known as the "Queen of the Prairie." Guthrie had its own water, mass transit, electricity, and underground parking for horse-drawn vehicles.

Voices from the past:

"Men knocked each other down as they rushed onward. Women shrieked and fell, fainting, only to be trampled and perhaps killed. Men, women, and horses were laying all over the prairie." **From a newspaper report, 1893**

Ingalls

*I**ngalls*** was founded in 1889 as an agricultural community. Crime came to town in form of the Doolin-Dalton gang, who spent money in the town.

Today, there isn't much going on in Ingalls, but you can see the stone monument dedicated to the heroes of the "Battle of Ingalls."

How to get to Ingalls:

Ingalls is located in north-central Oklahoma, about 9 miles east of Stillwater.

A moment in time:

Ingalls became a place for the Doolin-Dalton gang of outlaws to meet after bank or train robberies. The group gathered at the OK Hotel to play poker and enjoy the local entertainment. One evening, Marshal Red Lucas came into the hotel and played poker with the group. He became suspicious of their intentions and went back to Guthrie. Lucas got together with a group of lawmen and planned to capture the outlaws.

On the morning of September 1, 1893, the two groups met in the town of Ingalls. The Doolin gang consisted of Bill Doolin, Bill Dalton, Arkansas Tom Jones, Bitter Creek Bob Yocum, Dan

Clifton, George Newcomb, Tulsa Jack, Red Buck, and a few other lesser-known outlaws. The lawmen consisted of Ed Nix, A.H. Houston, Lafe Shadley, Red Lucas, James Masterson, Dick Speed, and a few others.

After a fierce, short gun battle, a 14 year-old boy was accidentally killed by the outlaws, along with another innocent citizen. Marshals Speed, Houston, and Shadley also were killed. Arkansas Tom surrendered, and the other Doolin-Dalton gang members were eventually captured or killed. The "Battle of Ingalls" would prove to be the last major event in the life of the Doolin-Dalton gang.
Morris

Oklahoma City

Oklahoma City is home to the wonderful First Americans Museum, also known as FAM. Artifacts and exhibits are housed in a spacious, architecturally beautiful building. As you walk through the museum, you will view clothing, textiles, weapons, and other artifacts of Native American life.

There is a fascinating Women as Warriors section detailing the many Native American women who fought in wars in the United States, at least as far back as the American Revolution. Another amazing part of the museum is the information about citizenship for Native Americans.   Some Native Americans became citizens when they received land in 1898. Others received citizenship when they were discharged from service after World War I. All Native Americans became citizens in 1924.

One of my favorite exhibits is a replica of a painted bison skull found in the Cooper Site in Harper County Oklahoma. The original is over 15,000 years old and is the oldest known painted object in North America.

This child's coat was collected in 1909 and was created from a lynx, an animal admired by the Comanche for its courage and stealth. FAM

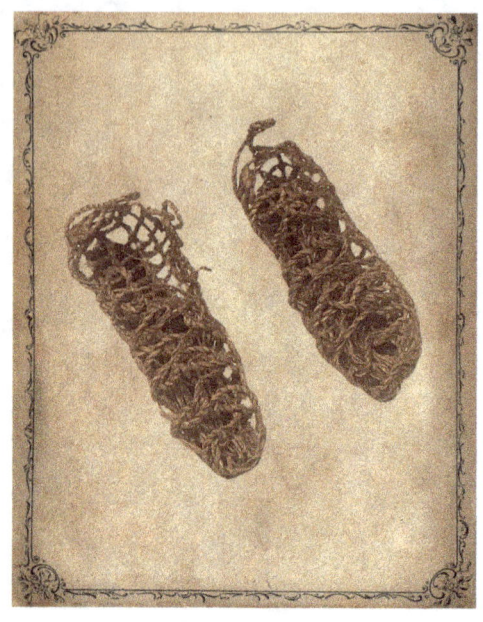

Another wonderful article of clothing is this pair of moccasins, made of tule, from the Modoc nation. These were collected in 1920.

There is a fascinating hide calendar, painted around 1900 from memory by Silver Horn of the Kiowa tribe. The painted figures are actual people, and can be identified by their shields and clothing.

Don't miss the British flag carried by Sawa Benashe (Yellow Hawk) during the war of 1812. Previously, Tecumseh carried the flag when he recruited other tribes to fight for the British against the US Army.

Outside the museum is a replica of an immense mound structure which you can walk around.

How to get to First Americans Museum:

The First Americans Museum is located at 659 American Indian Blvd, in Oklahoma City.

A word about the Osage Murders:

Osage County, Oklahoma, is the site of one of the most brutal, heartless incidents of Native American abuse and murder in U.S. history. It is unknown just how many Osage Native Americans were murdered during what was called the "Reign of Terror."

The Osage Nation were placed upon reservation land in Osage County, land everyone believed was worthless rock. Beneath that rock was one of the richest oil reserves in the world. The Osage were granted headrights, which were rights to a percentage of the minerals and oil found there.

In the 1920s, a string of murders began. The Osage were deemed unfit to manage their own affairs, so "guardians" were appointed to oversee each of the Osage member's wealth. One by one, Osage died mysteriously, either poisoned or shot by their guardians or underlings.

At least 60 Native Americans were murdered, and their wealth appropriated. Estimates are that several hundred Osage may have been murdered during the reign of terror. One of the principal murderers was William Hale, a well-known local businessman. Hale was eventually found guilty and sentenced for the murders, but there were other conspirators who were never caught.

Sacred Heart Mission

T he ***Sacred Heart Mission*** was founded in 1876 by Father Isidore Robot, a French Benedictine priest who journeyed into the area. He was accompanied by Brother Dominic Lambert, a resourceful man who helped make Sacred Heart Mission a reality.

The mission was built to benefit the Pottawatomie Indians. Over time, an abbey, church, a school, and log cabins were all built on the site. In 1901, fire spread through the mission, destroying many of the buildings. The glow from the fire could be seen from 30 miles away. Sacred Heart Mission

What remains of the Sacred Heart Mission lies on private land, with a locked gate. Fortunately, the caretaker and priest of Sacred Heart took me on a tour of the grounds.

Sacred Heart lies in a serene spot, and you can see the foundations of the old buildings including the abbey.

There are also cemeteries close by, one for the sisters, one for the priests, including Father Robot, and one for the Pottawatomie.

There is a two-story log structure, which is a reconstruction of what was the first home of Father Robot. This building would later serve as a cobbler's shop, among its many other functions.

The most spectacular building is the two-story stone structure, which was a bakery. When you step inside, you can see the recessed area in the wall which was the oven.

The bakery has a foundation stone that reads "1881."

How to get to Sacred Heart Mission:

The Sacred Heart Mission is located in the town of Konawa at 47943 Abbey Road.

Voices from the past:

"The bells that for many years entertained life in the neighboring country, resound no more-they are melted. The sweet strains of music, that rejoiced many hearts, have ceased-for the books are burned and the artists have gone away". **The Indian Advocate, March 1901.**

A word about the Oklahoma Dust Bowl:

The ***Dust Bowl*** was a series of prolonged storms occurring in the 1930s. Oklahoma was severely affected, along with Kansas, New Mexico, and Texas. The Dust Bowl was caused by several factors. An intense, prolonged drought. poor farming practices, and the Great Depression all contributed to more land being cultivated with crops which did not hold the soil in place. Winds over the dry fields caused "Black Blizzards" reaching 5 miles high. One storm carried away 350 million tons of dirt to the East Coast.

Fort Gibson

***F*ort Gibson Stockade** was established in 1824, by Colonel
Matthew Arbuckle of the 7th Infantry and was named for

Colonel George Gibson. The fort's purpose was to serve as a peacekeeper between the Osage and Cherokee nations.

It was constructed at a vital point where the Arkansas, Grand, and Verdigris rivers meet, to assist with river navigation and trade. Fort Gibson also made an excellent base for explorations further into the west.

The fort was abandoned temporarily in 1857, and then opened again during the Civil War. It became Fort Blunt and was the Union headquarters in Indian Territory.

As you walk around Fort Gibson, you can see both reconstructed buildings and original structures from the 1840s to 1870s.

You can also see the original well used by Jefferson Davis from 1833 to 1835. Fort Gibson was abandoned for good in 1890.

How to get to Fort Gibson Stockade:

Fort Gibson Stockade is located at 907 N. Garrison Ave, in Fort Gibson.

Ghost story:

There are reports of a female spirit who haunts the Fort Gibson cemetery. She is believed to be the spirit of a jilted bride who was left standing at the altar. She looked for the prospective groom and found him at Fort Gibson, in love with another woman. She shot the man, and became so sad about what she had done that she spent her nights crying by his grave. One night, she froze to death at the grave. She has now become a permanent resident of the cemetery.

Spiro Mounds

The **Spiro Mounds** is a mysterious archaeological site which has been heavily impacted by farming and looting of artifacts. Today, there are eight mounds of different sizes. The largest was used as both a temple and a burial mound. Archaeologists took over Spiro in 1935 and began systematic excavations which lasted until 1941. During this period, more artifacts were uncovered. Efforts were undertaken to locate the plundered artifacts and return them to Spiro.

Carbon-14 dating has provided dates of 818 to 1084 AD, with the culture reaching its peak 800-1100 AD. The complex was used by an estimated population of about 10,000 people from surrounding areas. A major prolonged drought happened between 1250 and

1450 AD. The Spiro people lost confidence in their leadership and gradually abandoned the area. By 1600, the people of Spiro were gone.

Evidence indicates that the mounds may have been constructed in specific alignment with celestial events or star positions. The elite class lived separately from the common people, typically nearer to the mounds.

Seven of the mounds at Spiro were used by the Great Sun, over a period of 400 years. The Great Sun was the leader of the people who lived at Spiro. When the leader died, the body was cleaned and clothed in ceremonial dress. The man's wife and servants were then executed and placed near the body. The home of the Great was destroyed and covered with dirt. The new leader's home was built on top of the previous one. When two to four leaders died, the mound stopped being used and another site for a mound was chosen.

The Craig Mound is a burial mound at Spiro and originally contained the remains of over 1100 leaders. 400 sets of remains were destroyed during mining in the area. About 700 sets of remains were uncovered during excavations. Artifacts including pipes, conch shells, copper plates and other objects were placed with the owner's body for use in the afterlife. Group burials were a common practice, where bodies would be cleaned of flesh, and the bones stored until a group burial occurred. Some group burials contained as many as 100 bodies. A clay crematorium was on the burial mound, indicating cremation was an important burial practice. Charred bone pieces were found in the crematorium.

The museum is wonderful, containing many artifacts, including these beads made of shell, and fashioned to resemble human finger bones. Artistic and cultural elements connect the temple mound builders in Oklahoma with other temple mound builders in Georgia and Alabama.

Copper was a status symbol for the people of Spiro. Copper ear spools and other ornaments can be seen in the museum.

Trade between the people of Spiro Mounds and other areas was widespread. reaching as far as the Great Lakes, Gulf of Mexico, Florida, and the Atlantic Coast as far as Virginia. Conch shell was another symbol of elite status in the Spiro world. This elaborate engraved shell is a replica. The original dates to 1200 to 1350 AD.

One of my favorite piece in the museum is this replica of a shell ornament known as a gorget. The original dates from 1200 to 1350 AD and was worn by one of the leaders of Spiro.

Another favorite is this replica of the Head of Tlanuwa, a mythical hawk creature. The original dates from 1200 to 1350 AD.

How to get to Spiro Mounds:

Spiro Mounds is located at 8154 First Street, in the town of Spiro.

A helpful timeline:

The various periods of occupation in early North America can be confusing. Don't be surprised if you read slightly different dates from other sources, but these are some general guidelines to know about:

The *Paleo-Indian Period*, from10,000 to 8500 BC, is characterized by hunting and gathering, and small family groups in temporary camps. Artifacts from this period include spears and darts.

The *Archaic Period*, from 8500 to 500 BC, is characterized by some cultivation, and small base settlements. Artifacts from this period include stone, shell, and copper items.

The *Early Woodland Period,* from 500 BC to 1 AD, is characterized by permanent villages, organization under a tribal or religious leader, and elite burials in mounds. Artifacts from this period include the addition of clay pottery.

The *Middle Woodland Period*, from 1 AD to 400 AD, is characterized by the introduction of maize, long-distance trade, and elite burials with precious objects. Burial mounds, platform mounds, and earthworks were built.

The *Late Woodland Period*, from 400 AD to 800 AD, is characterized by cultivated seed plants, large permanent villages, and use of the bow and arrow.

The *Early Mississippi Period*, from 800 AD to 1300 AD, is characterized by cultivation of corn, beans, and squash, with permanent villages and farming settlements. Temples and houses of leaders were built on mounds in major villages. Pottery and artistic forms were developed.

The *Late Mississippi Period*, from 1300 AD to 1700 AD, is characterized by towns enclosed in stockade walls, increased power among chiefs and religious leaders. Increased and more elaborate artistic representations on pottery, shells, and wood.

Fort Washita

F*ort Washita* construction was begun in 1842 and the fort was home to several rifle, artillery, infantry, and cavalry companies.

The purpose of the fort was to protect the Choctaw and Chickasaw Indian tribes from the plains indians and settlers moving west.

Fort Washita became more active during the California Gold Rush and Mexican War.

The fort also was occupied by Confederate forces during the Civil War.

How to get to Fort Washita:

Fort Washita is located at 3348 OK-199, in Durant.

Ghost Story:

There is a legend of Fort Washita, about the ghost of Aunt Jane, a woman who was decapitated. She is seen by some as a headless apparition in clothing from the 1800s. There are several tales about Aunt Jane. One is that she was a Union spy, caught and beheaded by the Confederates. Another is that she was the wife of an officer at Fort Washita who caught Jane and another man together and beheaded them both. Other paranormal happenings include hoofbeats and footsteps of soldiers, dark shadows, lights, and disembodied voices.

Washita Battlefield

Washita Battlefield is the site where the U.S. Army, led by Custer, attacked the winter camp of Cheyenne Peace Chief Black Kettle. It was a major battle of the Plains Indian

Wars. The scenery is stunning, but as you walk around the Washita Battlefield, there is a definite aura of sadness at the site.

How to get to Washita Battlefield:

The Washita Battlefield is located off Hwy. 47A, one mile west of Cheyenne, Oklahoma.

A moment in time:

On November 27, 1868, four U.S. Cavalry units, led by Custer, silently crept into the Cheyenne winter camp of Peace Chief Black Kettle. The night before, Black Kettle's wife wanted her husband to move their small camp closer to a larger Cheyenne camp for protection. Black Kettle decided to move their camp the next day, but the next day wasn't soon enough.

Custer and his 700 men attacked the camp. Black Kettle and his wife attempted to flee, but they were shot and killed. The fighting lasted about two hours, after which 30 to 60 Cheyenne warriors and 20 cavalry soldiers lay dead.

The soldiers killed about 875 Indian ponies, and destroyed their weapons, clothes, tipis, and everything of value to the Indians. Custer and his remaining men retreated with 53 captive women and children.

One of Custer's officers reported that Custer invited his officers to "avail themselves of the services of a captured squaw." Cheyenne stories tell of "comfort women" for the soldiers, and Custer himself. National Park Service

Profiles in history:

Chief Black Kettle was born in the Black Hills of South Dakota in 1803. He was a member of the Cheyenne tribe and an advocate for peace. Black Kettle was a member of the Council of 44 Chiefs and participated in several negotiations for peace. Chief Black Kettle and his band were relocated to Sand Creek. Black Kettle and his wife survived a massacre at Sand Creek, with Black Kettle's wife, Medicine Woman, receiving nine bullet and shrapnel wounds. Chief Black Kettle kept advocating for peace, right up until he was killed at the Battle of Washita in 1868.

George Armstrong Custer was born in Rumley, Ohio, Dec. 5, 1839. A former teacher, he went to US Military Academy, graduating in 1861. He served in the Civil War, as the youngest Union army general, and had many victories over confederates. He was said to have had horses shot out from under him, and only had one minor injury. Interestingly, Custer was court martialed for "deserting his post, failure to determine the welfare of some of his men, and using military equipment for personal reasons." He was suspended for one year without pay and reduced to the rank of captain. The story was, he went to defend his wife, who was staying at a nearby camp. Custer died in the battle of Little Bighorn June 25, 1876, 'following the orders of his commanding General Terry.

Voices from the past:

"All we ask is that we have peace with the whites. We want to hold you by the hand. You are our father." **Chief Black Kettle to Major Wynkoop at the Camp Weld Conference, September 28, 1864.**

A word about Native American conflict:

It is estimated that 800 treaties were negotiated between whites and Native Americans between the years of 1778 to 1871, and that less than 400 of the treaties were ratified.

Two-thirds of the treaties required the Native Americans to give up their ancestral lands. In exchange, they were promised annuities, which included food and other provisions. They were offered small amounts of land to live out their lives. In many cases, the government did not live up to their promises, and Native Americans were left starving and suffering.

Gold was found on Native American lands, so treaties were broken. Railroads came, and settlements began, dramatically increasing the number of whites. Conflicts broke out, with bands of warriors attacking white settlements. The attacks led to massacres of Native Americans by Custer and others.

Doaksville

Doaksville was once the largest town in southeastern Oklahoma during the 1840s and 1850s. It was home to members of the Choctaw and Chickasaw nations.

The town was at the crossroads of several military roads leading to Fort Gibson and Fort Smith. River transport was important to Doaksville, and connected it to major ports including New Orleans.

Doaksville began to decline during the Civil War, and the town was relocated into Fort Towson in 1900.

You begin an exploration of Doaksville by entering the Doaksville Cemetery, where the first settlers of Doaksville were buried in the early 1800s. Interestingly, one of the gravestones came from Lamar County, Texas, and was transported by wagon. Another came from New Orleans and was transported by steamboat.

The jail was comprised of three cells and had outer walls which were two feet thick. Three types of punishment were handed down to prisoners of the Choctaw nation, fines, whippings, and death.

Artifacts found in the area of the mercantile store included fine
English ceramics, manufactured by Davenport, with a date of 1849,
indicating Doaksville residents enjoyed some luxuries.

Doaksville had three wells, one of which had a stone pavement surrounding it. In the Choctaw nation, everyone was equal, so anyone could draw water from the wells.

The Doaksville Hotel was run by Colonel David Folsom of the Choctaw nation during the 1840s. It was a large building measuring 41 feet and most likely had two stories. Pieces of plates, bowls, cups, and glass windows were found in this area.

One area which was excavated contained evidence of having been burned in a fire. Platters and tableware were found during the excavations, indicating this area may have been a residence or a tavern which served food.

How to get to Doaksville:

Doaksville is located on Fort Towson Cemetery Red Road, in Fort Towson.

Voices from the past:

" The location of Doaksville is very unpleasant, especially during the wet season. It stands mostly upon two hills, jutting out into a narrow valley, through which flows a small stream. The soil is sticky clay, which renders the streets at times almost impassible. On account of the uncertain stay of a majority of the inhabitants, no public interest is felt in making improvements." **Rev. P.P. Brown, 1847**

A word about the Trail of Tears:

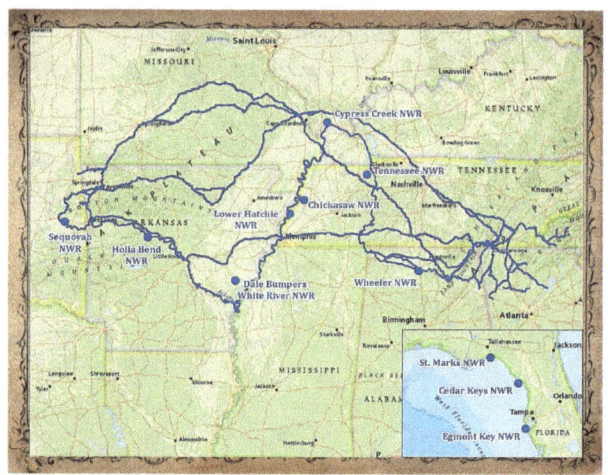

The Trail of Tears is one of the most shameful events in the relationship between Native American tribes and the U.S. government. It happened as a result of the Indian Removal Act of 1830. The Trail of Tears refers to the forced removal and relocation of thousands of Native Americans. Tribes impacted included the Cherokee, Choctaw, Chickasaw, Moscogee, and Seminole. These tribes were removed from their native homelands in Tennessee, Alabama, North Carolina, and Georgia and forced to walk west, eventually reaching Oklahoma. Over 10,000 Native Americans died on the 1200-mile journey, facing starvation and disease.

Random Thoughts

What History Means to Me

F irst, let me start by sharing with you my opinion of what history isn't. History is not a collection of random dates, names, and places for you to memorize. History is not a dry and uninteresting class you have to pass to graduate.

I believe history is a tangible thing. You can actually *feel* history in the places you go, and the sights you see. I remember walking up to the Acropolis in Athens. I looked down at the well-worn marble steps and wondered about how many ancient philosophers had climbed these very steps, thousands of years ago.

You don't have to go far away to experience the *feeling* of history. If you are lucky enough to live in an old house, you may experience history in your own surroundings. You might say to yourself, *"If only these walls could talk."*

During my travels across the United States, I *felt* history in many, many places. If you travel across the country like I did, you will *feel* the wonderful history of our beautiful country for yourself, and you will never be the same. You will discover what it means to be an American.

Why I travel, and why you should too:

I decided to travel across the country by car because I wanted to rediscover America. When I first set out to explore the history of our country, I wanted to find out why America is the greatest country on earth, and what it means to be an American.

The politics of these United States can be frightening and polarizing. I prefer to focus on what unites us, not what divides us. What unites us is we all live in a spectacularly beautiful country, with warm, wonderful people.

I began my journey five years ago, starting out in my Honda CRV. I soon realized I loved the lifestyle, so now I travel in a small RV. From my small RV, I look out on a country with a unique and colorful, multicultural tapestry, unlike any other country on earth.

I have a degree in Archaeology, and a passion for all things archaeological. I love history, with a side love of paleontology. It is these three passions that I set my trip agenda around. I set out to discover the archaeological sites, history, and paleontological world of our country.

As I travel and write my books, I get asked all the time, especially by women, "What is it like to travel by yourself? Aren't you scared?" The truth is, I believe everyone should do what I did. It's a wonderful way to discover our country, and to rediscover yourself. The truth is, I'm scared not to travel. Traveling allows you to get to know yourself, in ways not possible when sitting on the couch watching TV.

We tend to spend a lot of our lives tuning out the world and our place within it. When you travel, you are quite literally forced to deal with your own thoughts, emotions, and feelings. You can discover yourself while traveling. You can come to understand what makes you who you are, and how you can perhaps become a better person. Above all, traveling gives you mental clarity to figure out how to live with intent. It's a way to guide your life, not just wait for things to happen.

Travel Tips & Stuff

What You Need to Know

How to get started:

P lanning your trip should be one of the most exciting things
about it. You want to be spontaneous, but it is also very wise
to plan your route, so you can take full advantage of all the time
and miles you will invest.

- First, decide your passions. If you love airplanes, trains, or
  old vehicles, plan your trip around that. If you love gardens
  or architecture, seek that out as the focus of your trip.

- Next, read and research areas of the country that will let
  you enjoy what you are interested in.

- Make a list by state and city or town, of what you want to
  see.

- Take your handy road atlas and locate the areas on the
  pages.

- Make a tentative route plan, so you have an idea of where
  you are going.

Travel tip: Avoid trying to plan your trip down to a schedule of days, hours, or minutes. On a road trip, it will be virtually impossible to know where you will be on any given day. If you adhere to a schedule, you are more likely to stress out, and less likely to actually enjoy yourself, which is the whole point.

What you need:

You need to bring along a sense of adventure and a curious mind. You need to ditch the idea of always being on a schedule, and live a little more spontaneously to thoroughly enjoy yourself. Things will happen as you travel, both good things and bad things, and you need to prepare your mind and your soul for day-to-day changes.

So much of our lives are planned out. Between growing up, going to school, finding a career, marriage, kids, or whatever, people have lost much of the ability to be spontaneous. But you must take spontaneity on the trip with you, because you may make detours along the way to see something really spectacular.

So, for the practical stuff you need:

A great vehicle-I am now five years into the trip and have swapped out my Honda CRV for a small RV, just under 20 feet. I go small because I see humongous RVs on the road, towing a car behind, and all I can think of is, they can't go just anywhere. They are too big. Bad gas mileage, cumbersome to drive, slow, and not agile like my small RV. So, I encourage you, if you want to go car or RV camping and be able to go on remote dirt roads, get an agile vehicle, and small RVs are great.

Travel tip: Don't be afraid to do some modifications to your vehicle. I have made many alterations to my RV, including changing the plumbing, which used to be a mere 4 inches off of the ground, so I would break it all the time. It's now encased in my outside storage compartment. I am also a minimalist, so I have jettisoned anything I won't use or don't love. Don't be afraid to get rid of unnecessary stuff.

An awesome camera that you know inside and out. I use a Nikon and it takes wonderful pictures. Don't skimp on a camera, and don't think a cellphone camera is all you need, because you want the best for your beautiful photos.

Window shades-the best ones are magnetic so you just place them against your windows and they cling to them, obscuring the view inside your car. I also have magnetic window screens, so I can leave my windows down with no bugs!

Battery operated fans and lights-these are important, so you don't have to rely on your house batteries for light and cooling options.

Portable air compressor-this little gem plugs into your cigarette lighter and will inflate your tires if you have a flat. Make sure the air compressor can reach to all of your tires, including your rear tires.

Portable battery charger and power bank-mine comes with battery cables and the power bank, yet once inside the case, it is small enough to put in your glove compartment. This little item, unfortunately, I have had to use, and it saved me.

Portable generator-I have two gas powered generators on the back of my RV, which are hooked together with a coupling unit. I have an interior generator, but after much expense and multiple repairs, it still doesn't work. Now I have generators which will run everything, including AC, and I can maintain them myself.

All season clothing-you never know what different states will bring for weather, so take hot weather and cold weather clothes, and a fair amount of shoes appropriate for hiking, or walking, sandals, and slippers, which are nice at night. Also take along a pair of cheap rubber flip-flops to wear in the public showers you might go into.

Your own pillows-I like my own pillows, so I don't wake up with neck cramps, especially after sleeping in the car.

Sleeping bag and cozy blankets-you want to stay warm and layering is everything.

Warm hat, warm socks, and fuzzy jammies to keep you warm for cold nights sleeping in the car.

A great road atlas, and great guidebooks-get one that's easy to read, with great pictures. For a road atlas, just get one that is easy to read.

A word about photography:

Along with a great camera, you need to have a great eye. This is easier than it sounds once you have worked with your camera and are comfortable taking pictures with it. I am not a professional photographer, but I like my pictures and other people do too.

These are my tips for taking great pictures:

- Experiment with taking both horizontal and vertical shots.

- Don't always put the subject of the photo in the middle of the photograph.

- This one is important: pay attention to the foreground, and if possible, have something, a plant or whatever, in the foreground to help give the photo dimension and depth.

- This one is important too: turn around often to see the view you just came from. I do this quite often and some of my best pictures have resulted from when I turned around and took the shot.

You can also take a mental photo. Place an image in your mind that you can call upon later. Use all of your senses to see, hear, smell, and maybe even to taste, what is around you. You have the means to fully experience your surroundings, and that is very important to a traveler. When you take a mental photo, be sure to jot down quick little details about what you saw, heard, smelled, or tasted, so you can jog your memory later.

And last, but not least...don't be posing in front of everything, everywhere, to show that you actually went somewhere. Most people want to see themselves in your photo and be mentally transported there, but they can't if you are there already.

To camp or not to camp:

Car or RV camping is great. I prefer it to sleeping on the cold, hard ground in a tent. I can lock the doors, put my window shades up and be cozy for the night.

Some people camp in a Walmart parking lot and feel safe. I do not. I believe that if you are in a busy area, you are more likely to be confronted by a nut job who may bother you. Nothing against Walmart, and many Walmart stores don't allow overnight parking. I don't go for rest areas either because they have a track record of incidents happening to people in rest areas, especially women travelers.

I have come to love casino parking lots. I enjoy gambling, so for a little money, many casinos will provide overnight stays if you gamble a little inside the casino. I also do a lot of boondocking, because it's free, and I believe you are safer parked out in the middle of nowhere in the dark.

I also enjoy camping in state or national campgrounds, wildlife sanctuaries, and fairgrounds.

A word about safety:

When you are a woman traveling alone, it's critical to keep a low profile. Don't tell people you are traveling alone, where you are staying, or any other personal information.

I don't go to bars or get drunk. I'm not preaching but you are on your own, in a city or town you've never been to, and you don't know anyone, so it's not the time to lose control of what you are doing. When you are in control, you are better able to decide which people you want to get to know better.

Travel tip: If you feel vulnerable traveling alone, that's OK. Vulnerability is part of passion, and traveling is a passionate thing to do. You can put one of those family stickers on your vehicle to indicate to others that you are not traveling alone, which can help you feel more secure.

Maintain your connections:

When you are traveling alone, there is a definite sense of disconnection. It feels almost like you are the only one in the world, traveling through space and time. That's why it's critical to keep your connections to loved ones active.

Be on Facebook while you are traveling. You may not have internet a lot of the time, or the internet will be poor. Consider paying to have your phone be a hotspot. It's a little bit of money per month, but it's worth it and has saved me from being without internet. I love the convenience of it, and you will too.

Plan your journey around visiting family members or friends you haven't seen for a long time, or people that are good friends. When you see people you know, it will ground you, so you can continue traveling.

Check in by phone with loved ones. They worry about you, and it's good for both of you to stay connected no matter where you are.

Consider traveling with a pet. I now travel with my 12 year-old sheltie Rosie, after losing my beloved sheltie, Sadie. Rosie is a wonderful companion. She is also an excellent watchdog, and barks her head off at other dogs and people.

Travel tip: One of the easiest and best ways I stay connected while traveling is to offer to take a photo for someone I don't know. Many couples, families, or singles would love to have more pictures of themselves traveling. It's an easy and quick way to have a connection with a fellow traveler, and it's good manners too.

Practical matters:

You need to have an address to send your mail to. Keep in touch with whomever is nice enough to do this for you.

You will also need to come back occasionally to register your car, vote, go to doctor visits, and take care of any other business. You can't leave it all behind, as tempting as that may be.

Bad things that happened:

I have had a few problems, mostly associated with my RV. I bought an older model, vintage 1999, and I have had to do a few repairs.

My worst experience came when I took my rig in to a shop in Spokane, Washington (who shall remain nameless.) All I needed was an oil change. I got the oil change and was about an hour south of town on a Friday at 4:30, when my engine blew.

I was in the middle of the eastern Washington prairie, many miles from the nearest town. All I could do was watch my oil drain out onto the Interstate. I can't help but think it was associated with my oil change, but I couldn't prove it. The moral of this story is: DON'T LET JUST ANYONE WORK ON YOUR VEHICLE.

Good things that happened:

I have met many great people on my travels, from all walks of life. I have also learned not to judge people. I have met numerous homeless people who are often just wanting a kind word, and not to be treated like dirt.

People have mistaken me for a homeless person, and I too, have been treated like dirt. When I can, I try to help people and be kind to them. Most of the time, they smile and reciprocate. You will always meet people who are unkind, but they are just as likely to be driving a huge expensive rig, or to be homeless.

We are all Americans, and we are all part of the human race. When you meet people across the country, you realize just how important it is to get to know your fellow citizens, and learn more about how they view the world and our country.

I have to give a special shout-out to the many dedicated people, often volunteers, who staff our state and national parks and monuments. They work tirelessly to ensure the health of our natural resources, and help travelers enjoy their visit. The same is true of the many people who staff the museums in small towns and large cities. They enjoy history, like I do, and it shows in their smiles.

Along with wonderful people, I have seen an America that is spectacularly beautiful, with open prairies, majestic mountains, and crystal clear rivers. I have seen a small fraction of the history of our country. I have seen the memorials to the brave people who shaped our country. I have fallen in love with America in a way that was not possible sitting in my living room. People ask me, "would I do it again?" The answer comes easily, "Yes, in a heartbeat."

Bibliography & Further Reading

America Revealed, 2012, LIFE Books.

Donovan, Jim. *A Terrible Glory: Custer and the Little Bighorn-the Last Great Battle of the American West*. Back Bay Books, 2009.

Finch, etc. al.., Jackie. *Eyewitness Travel USA*. DK Publishing, 2017.

Glassman, Steve, *It Happened on the Santa Fe Trail*, Morris Book Publishing, 2008.

Grann, David, *Killers of the Flower Moon*, Vintage Books, 2017.

Hill, William, *The Oregon Trail Yesterday and Today*, Caxton Press, 2016.

Mayo, Matthew, *Haunted Old West*, Rowman & Littlefield, 2012.

Morris, John, *Ghost Towns of Oklahoma*, University of Oklahoma Press, 1978.

National Park Service, *National Parks of the Midwest.*

Ricksecker, Mike, *Ghosts and Legends of Oklahoma*, Schiffer Publishing, 2011.

Silverberg, Robert , *The Mound Builders,* Ohio University Press, 1970.

Wagner, Tricia Martineau. *It Happened on the Oregon Trail: Remarkable Events That Shaped History*. GPP, 2014.

Index
Referenced by Sections

A word about the Trail of Tears-see Doaksville

B

Battle of Ingalls-see Ingalls

Black blizzards-see Sacred Heart Mission

Black Kettle, Cheyenne Peace Chief-see Washita Battlefield

Bonfils, F.C.-see Guthrie

Brown, Rev. P.P.-see Doaksville

Busey, Gary-see Famous Citizens of Oklahoma

C

California Gold Rush-see Fort Washita

Camp Weld Conference-see Washita Battlefield

Chaney, Lon Jr.-see Famous Citizens of Oklahoma

Cherokee Nation-see Fort Gibson

Chickasaw tribe-see Fort Washita, Doaksville

Choctaw tribe-see Fort Washita, Doaksville

Civil War-see Fort Gibson, Fort Washita, Washita Battlefield, Doaksville

Clifton, Dan-see Ingalls

Cooper Site-see Oklahoma City

Y

About the Author

Julie Bettendorf is a world traveler with a degree in archaeology and a background in history. She has traveled extensively throughout Egypt, Central America, South America, Europe, and the United Kingdom, visiting archaeological and historical sites all along the way.

Currently, Julie is traveling around the US visiting ghost towns, ancient rock art sites, and archaeological wonders as part of research for her ongoing historical travel series entitled *Wandering Woman*. Wandering Woman is a set of state-by-state guides, full of photographs, historical anecdotes, and unique tips to help other women travel and explore solo across the US by car or RV. Julie enjoys writing freelance blogs, traveling frequently with her two adult children, and hiking outdoors with her faithful dog companion Rosie.

Also By Julie Bettendorf

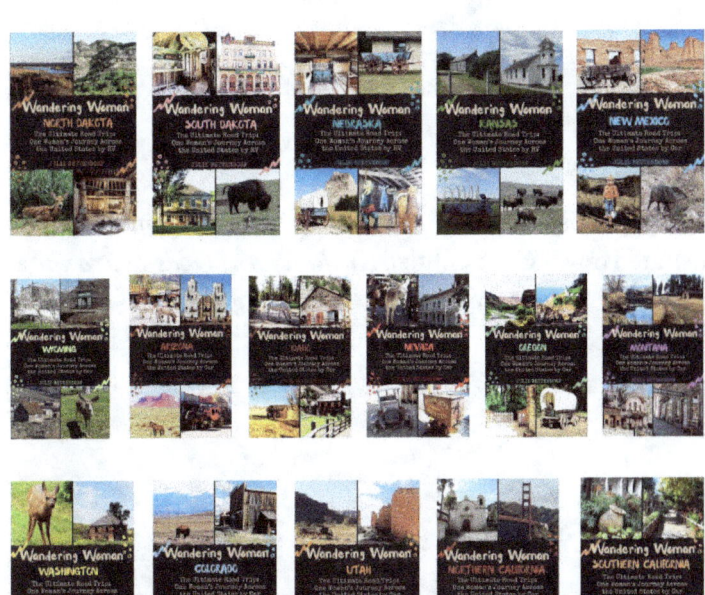

Wandering Woman: Oklahoma is the most recent book in the *Wandering Woman Travel Series*. Additional books in the series including, *Wandering Woman: Montana, Colorado, Nevada, Utah, Idaho, Oregon, Washington, Arizona, New Mexico, Wyoming, Kansas, Nebraska, South Dakota, North Dakota, Northern California*, and *Southern California* are available in ebook and paperback.

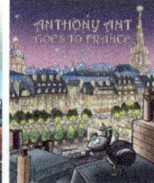

Julie has published two children's books in an ongoing, beautifully illustrated travel series entitled *Anthony Ant Goes to France* and *Anthony Ant Goes to Egypt*.